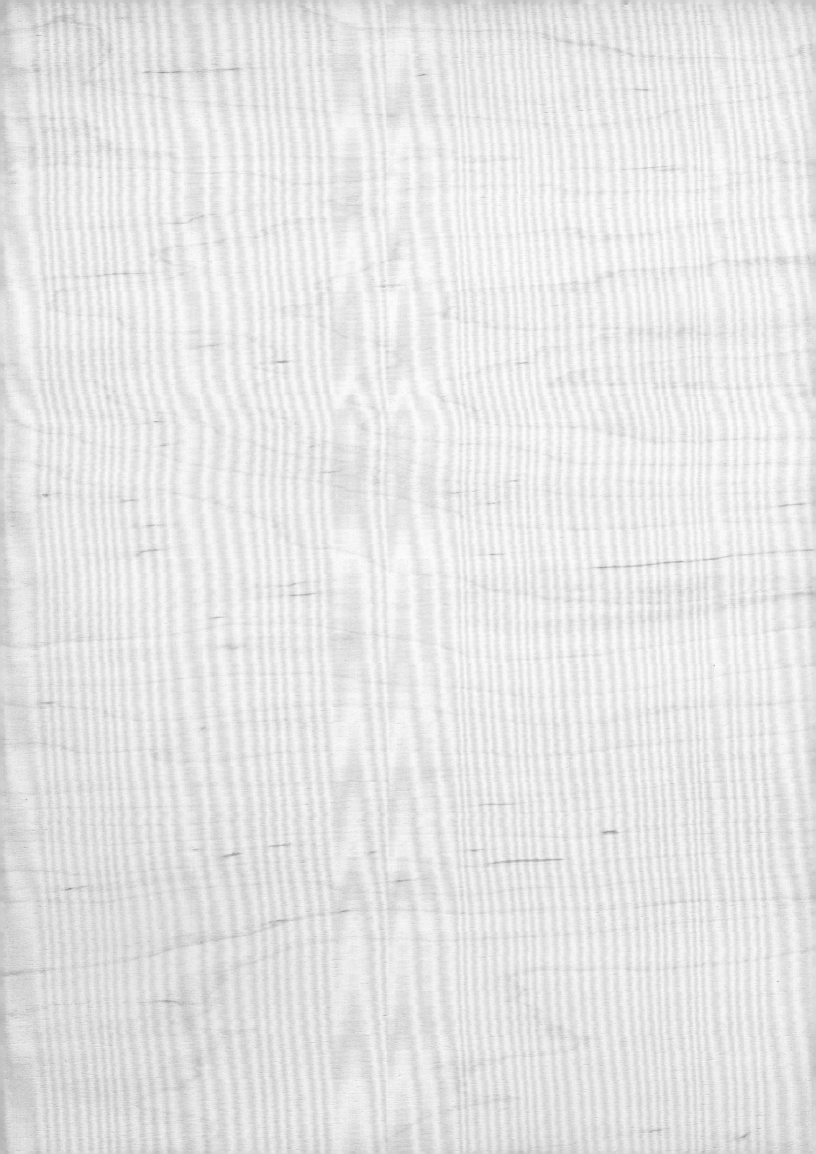

Brave Baby Hummingbird

Written by Sy Montgomery • Illustrated by Tiffany Bozic

A Paula Wiseman Book

Simon & Schuster Books for Young Readers • New York London Toronto Sydney New Delhi

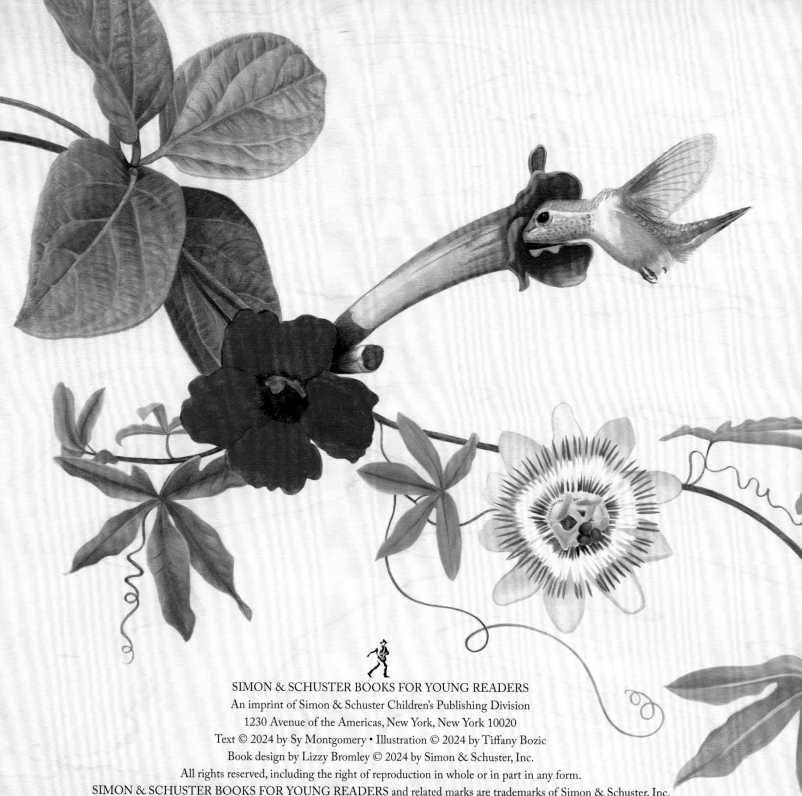

SIMON & SCHUSTER BOOKS FOR YOUNG READERS
An imprint of Simon & Schuster Children's Publishing Division
1230 Avenue of the Americas, New York, New York 10020
Text © 2024 by Sy Montgomery • Illustration © 2024 by Tiffany Bozic
Book design by Lizzy Bromley © 2024 by Simon & Schuster, Inc.
SIMON & SCHUSTER BOOKS FOR YOUNG READERS and related marks are trademarks of Simon & Schuster, Inc.
Simon & Schuster: Celebrating 100 Years of Publishing in 2024
For information about special discounts for bulk purchases, please contact Simon & Schuster Special Sales
at 1-866-506-1949 or business@simonandschuster.com.
The Simon & Schuster Speakers Bureau can bring authors to your live event. For more information or to book an event,
contact the Simon & Schuster Speakers Bureau at 1-866-248-3049 or visit our website at www.simonspeakers.com.
The text for this book was set in Adobe Caslon and Pencil Pete. • The illustrations for this book were rendered in acrylic paint on wood.
Manufactured in China • 1123 SCP • First Edition
2 4 6 8 10 9 7 5 3 1
Library of Congress Cataloging-in-Publication Data
Names: Montgomery, Sy, author. | Bozic, Tiffany, illustrator. • Title: Brave baby hummingbird / Sy Montgomery ; illustrated by Tiffany Bozic.
Description: First edition. | New York : Simon & Schuster Books for Young Readers, [2024]
"A Paula Wiseman Book"—Title page. | Includes bibliographical references. | Audience: Ages 4–8 | Audience: Grades 2–3
Summary: "The story of a hummingbird's early life and how they make their way into the world"—Provided by publisher.
Identifiers: LCCN 2023006375 (print) | LCCN 2023006376 (ebook) | ISBN 9781665918497 (hardcover) | ISBN 9781665918503 (ebook)
Subjects: LCSH: Hummingbirds—Anecdotes—Juvenile literature. | Wildlife rehabilitation—Anecdotes—Juvenile literature.
Classification: LCC QL696.A558 M69 2024 (print) | LCC QL696.A558 (ebook) | DDC 598.7/64—dc23/eng/20230420
LC record available at https://lccn.loc.gov/2023006375
LC ebook record available at https://lccn.loc.gov/2023006376

In memory of Dianne Taylor-Snow,
my companion for so many migrations.
—S. M.

For my sister, Sheree: my first friend, drawing buddy,
and fellow crawdad wrangler. Thank you for being my rock
throughout this journey, and for laughing through
tears with me. You bring light to dark places.

And if you love hummingbirds too, this is also for you.
—T. B.

I am one of the lightest birds in the sky.

Yet I am also one of the fastest.

I am tiny. But I can fly a very long way.

I am mostly made of air—like a bubble wrapped in feathers. Yet I am superstrong.

I am only a little hummingbird.

But I can do things no other bird can!

My first year isn't easy. My older sister and I hatch, two days apart, from eggs as small as navy beans. We're born the size of bumblebees. We snuggle in a soft nest no bigger than a quarter. Every twenty minutes, we wait for the breeze.

Food! We eat our fill many times a day.
One day there is no breeze at all. By nighttime,
we are scared, cold, and hungry.

But help comes in the morning.
Soon we are safe and warm.
But we are still hungry.

Ah! We feel the breeze again.
We open our beaks. Food!

Every twenty minutes of every day,
the breeze returns.

We open our eyes.

We start growing feathers.

One day my older sister stands up tall
in our nest—and beats her wings!

"You're growing stronger every day," a Voice says to us. "I'm not
a mother hummingbird, but I've spent ten years learning how
to help orphans like you. Soon you will learn to fly!"

Two days later I try out my own wings. Fun!
My sister learns a new skill. Perching!
I want to be just like her.

Every few days we move our quarters. My older
sister is always ahead of me. In each new basket,
we learn a new lesson: hopping from branch
to branch. Sipping nectar from flowers. Flying.
Catching fruit flies.

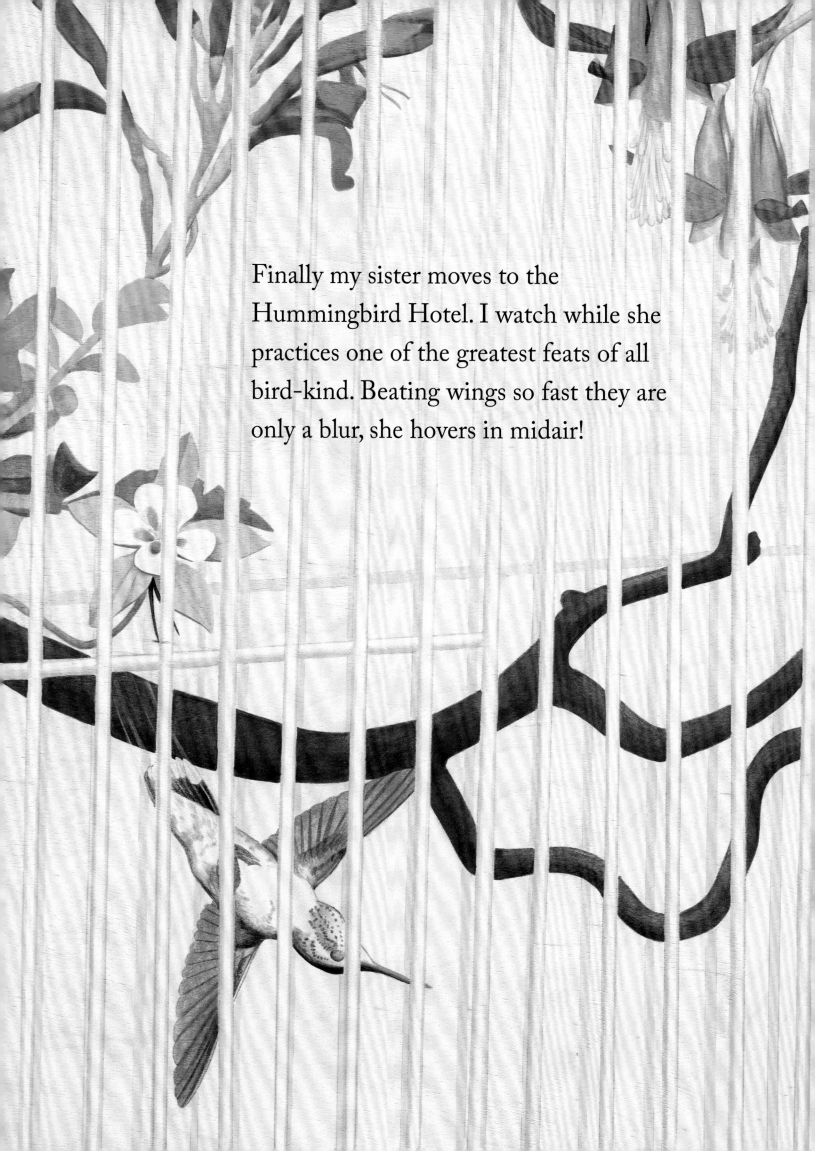

Finally my sister moves to the Hummingbird Hotel. I watch while she practices one of the greatest feats of all bird-kind. Beating wings so fast they are only a blur, she hovers in midair!

Only hummingbirds can hover. While hovering, we hummingbirds can also fly forward AND backward, up and down. We can even fly upside down! No other bird can do that.

One day the door to the Hummingbird Hotel swings open. "You're a wild bird now!" the Voice says. My sister darts out and dives down a slope to a bay tree. Then she disappears.

From inside the smaller flight cage on the patio, I search for my sister. I see plenty of other hummingbirds. They are sipping nectar from feeders, catching bugs in the compost pile, hovering while poking their long beaks into the many flowers in the yard.

They spend as much time chasing one another away from the food as they do eating!

But where is my sister?

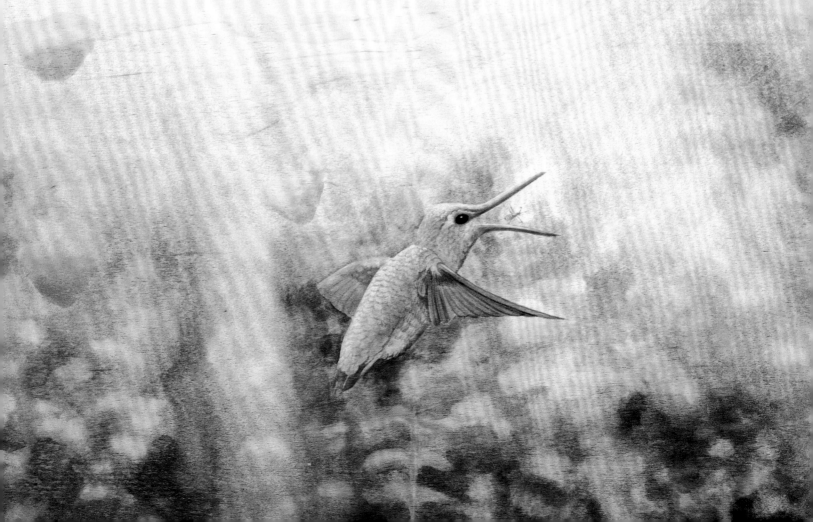

A flash of green zips by. "That's her!" says the Voice. My sister heads for the corner feeder, flying faster than ever before!

Another larger flash of green follows. A different hummingbird is chasing my sister away from the food! We watch the bigger bird hover while sipping the nectar. A flash of green shoots out of a tree; the big hummer leaves in a hurry.

"Welcome back!" the Voice says to my sister. "You're brave!" My sister hovers by the feeder, enjoying a drink.

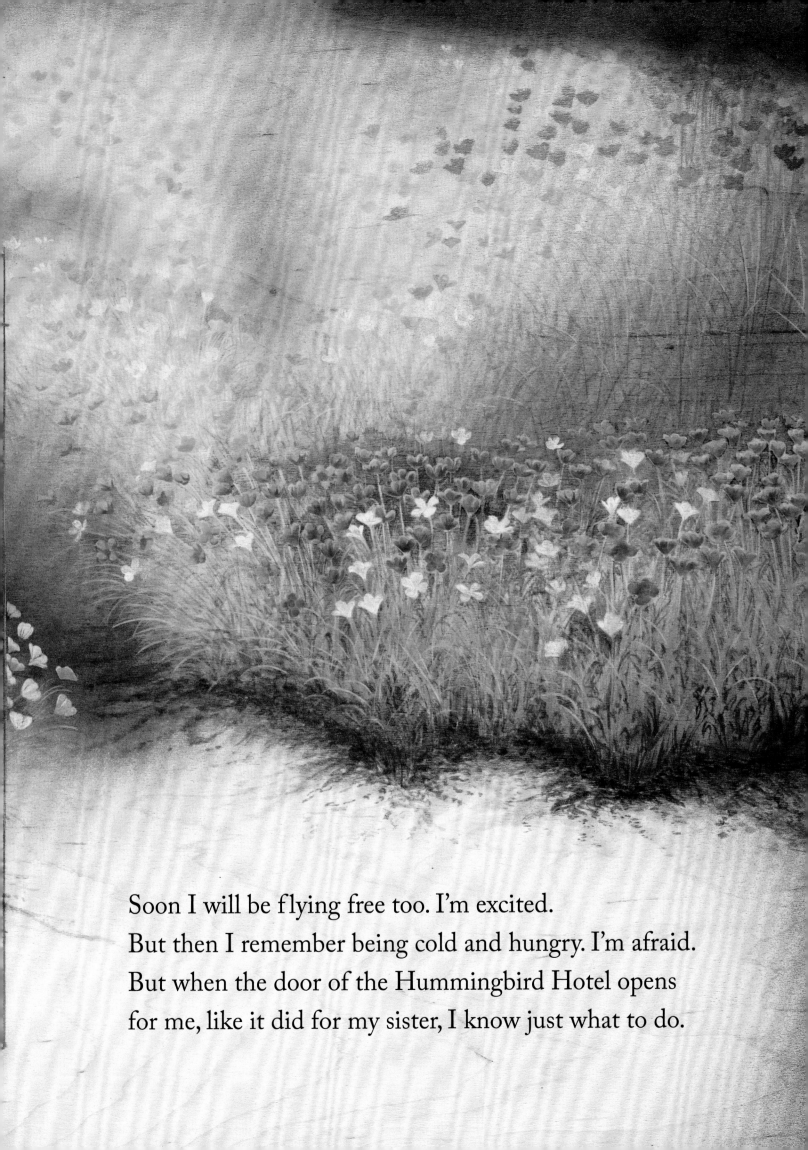

Soon I will be flying free too. I'm excited.
But then I remember being cold and hungry. I'm afraid.
But when the door of the Hummingbird Hotel opens
for me, like it did for my sister, I know just what to do.

Our wings are strong. Our eyes are sharp.
Because we are so small, because we are so light,
we have powers no other birds have.

I practice my hover: up and down,
back and forth, even upside down!

I drink from all the feeders in the backyard.
I hunt for yummy bugs in the compost pile.

I visit all the flowers.
I especially like the red ones.

Sometimes my sister and I hover
near the Voice, just to say hello.
But soon we are off again. And in
two days' time, we get the same
idea: it's time to leave. Somehow
we know just where to go.

We fly south, over vast mountains.
We fly just above the treetops. We fly
low over water. We stop to catch bugs.
We sip nectar from flowers we have never
seen before. We sleep very deeply each
night in the trees. Then we fly again.

Finally we arrive. We have never been to this place, but we know: this is where we stop.

It's warm and sunny. Flowers and bugs are
everywhere. So are other hummingbirds—
more kinds than we've ever seen before:
hummingbirds with blue heads. Hummingbirds
with purple throats. Hummingbirds with golden
tails. It's a good place to stay. But only for a while.
In December, once again, I know just what to do:

I leave first. I fly low, crossing over the water. I fly just above the treetops. I fly, day after day, over the vast mountains. For our size, we hummingbirds complete some of the longest flights of any bird in the sky.

Now my grown-up feathers are brighter.
My throat now bears a glittering patch
of orange, like a coppery fire.

When the female hummingbirds arrive,
I will impress them all. I will fly high and
dive for 100 feet—faster, for my size, than
any other kind of bird on Earth!

I will hover in front of the
female and fly side to side,
flashing my beautiful throat.

My sister arrives a few days after me. She will select a mate of her own, a handsome male whose bright orange throat catches her eye.

Then, hidden in the leaves of a climbing vine, she will build a nest, just like the one we shared when we were little: small as a coin, lined with thistledown. In it she will lay two eggs.

My sister and I zip around the yard, sipping nectar, catching bugs. The Voice sets out fresh nectar in feeders each morning. Sometimes we hover near her face. "Is that you?" she asks. She may never know for sure.

But *we* know: thanks to her, though we were once cold, alone, and frightened; though we are small, and light, and delicate,

now we have grown
to rule the sky.

Author's Note:

Dear Reader,

This is the story of two real baby hummingbirds
I was privileged to meet. As you see in this book,
hummingbirds have amazing powers. But they are
also fragile creatures, and only trained and licensed
rehabilitators have the specialized know-how to care
for them if they are injured or orphaned. This book
is not meant to encourage people to try to care for
hummingbirds that are hurt or abandoned. Leave that
to the experts. But there's lots you CAN do to help
them! Look in the back of the book to see how you
can make your yard a safe haven for these beautiful
but beleaguered little birds. Plant a pollinator garden.
Learn what to do if you do find an injured bird. And
find out more about the hummingbirds' amazing
migrations, the organizations studying their lives, and
the charities working to protect the hummingbirds and
their habitats.

Your friend,

Sy

Hummingbird Highlights:

The world is graced with more than 330 species of hummingbird. All of them live in either North, Central, or South America.

Hummingbirds are the tiniest of birds. The very biggest one, called the Andean giant hummingbird, is not a giant at all. It's only eight inches long. The smallest is the bee hummingbird of Cuba, which is about two inches long and weighs less than a dime. It's the smallest bird in the world.

Hummingbirds are the lightest birds in the sky. Like most birds, their bones are hollow; their feathers weigh more than their skeletons. Their bodies are full of air sacs. There are nine of these air sacs inside the hummingbird, in addition to their two hardworking lungs.

Because they are slight and tiny, hummingbirds can do things other birds cannot. They are the speediest birds in the world. Everything they do is fast! While hummingbirds hover, their wings flap so quickly a person sees only a blur. Some species beat their wings eighty times every second. At rest, the average hummingbird breathes 250 times a minute (a minute during which a resting person breathes only twelve to twenty times!). During the migration, their hearts can beat 1,260 times a minute—the highest heart rate of all species.

The fastest bird on Earth—if you account for body size—is the male Allen's hummingbird, the kind in this book. To impress a female, he plunges from the sky at sixty feet per second—faster, per body length, than a space shuttle screams down through Earth's atmosphere!

And little hummingbirds fly a long way. Allen's hummingbirds in this book migrate 2,200 miles from the San Francisco area to central Mexico. (The rufous hummingbird holds the record for the longest trip, per body length, of any bird: 3,900 miles, from Alaska to Mexico.)

Helping Hummingbirds:

Here's how to help hummingbirds in your own yard.

—Plant flowers hummingbirds enjoy. Bee balm, cardinal flower, and salvia are a few. They especially love bright red tubular flowers. A hummingbird typically visits 1,500 flowers every day.

—Keep a compost pile. In addition to nectar, hummingbirds need the protein they get from eating 600–700 little insects a day. Your compost pile is a great way to attract yummy bugs.

—Offer fresh nectar in feeders every day. Be sure it's fresh, and never dye it red; spoiled nectar can make hummers sick, and red dye can hurt their feathers.

—Keep your cats indoors. Rehabilitators report that being caught by cats is the top reason most species of wild birds come to rehabilitators needing care. Most hummingbirds caught by cats die because they are so small and fragile.

—Don't use pesticides or insecticides on your lawn or flowers. This can poison hummingbirds.

—If a baby hummingbird falls from a nest, put it back. The mother won't reject it because you have handled it.

—If you see hummingbird babies alone in a nest, they probably are not orphans. The mother leaves the nest up to 100 times a day to search for nectar and bugs to feed the nestlings, and may spend only three to five seconds with the babies each time she returns to feed them. Watch the nest—without looking away—for an entire hour for the mother's return to be sure that the mother is really gone.

—No mom? Immediately call your local wildlife rehabilitator. To find one in your area, contact the National Wildlife Rehabilitators Association here: ahnow.org.

Many organizations are working hard to learn more about hummingbirds so they can protect them. Here are some that would appreciate your support:

The International Hummingbird Society provides hummingbird information and endangered species protection: hummingbirdsociety.org.

The Hummingbird Monitoring Society combines scientific research with community involvement to create projects and services that benefit hummingbirds: hummonnet.org.

Operation Ruby Throat offers information about attracting and studying hummingbirds, feeding, banding, and student projects: rubythroat.org.